A Brief Introduction to the Economics of Greed and Exploitation

A philosophical critique of modern economic practices with suggested solutions for improvements

Ashok Malhotra
Ph. D., UBC Canada

A Brief Introduction to the Economics of Greed and Exploitation

© **By Ashok Malhotra** 2014

Primarily based on earlier blog articles by the author ever since the financial crisis of 2008

First Revision: September 2014

ISBN-13:
978-1495448195

ISBN-10:
1495448193
ISBN by CreateSpace
USA

A Brief Introduction

Contents

Chapter		Page
1	How the Wealth of our World is distributed	5
2	When to Tax the Rich and when not to	11
3	Inflation is like stealing from the Poor	17
4	The Rule of Ten	27
5	Proportional Tax – A New Method of Corporate Taxation	35
6	The Paradox of Modern Life and Economy	47
7	Fixing the Banks	53
8	Future of World Economies	59
9	A Spiritual view of Economy and Recession	65

Acknowledgement

This author is grateful to Aaron Heslehurst of BBC World News and other economic news correspondents from around the world for having kept him abreast of international economic news.

A Brief Introduction

1

How the Wealth of our World is distributed

We know from history that in the past, much of the world's wealth was held by a few rich and powerful kings and emperors. Has that changed now? Have you wondered how the world's wealth is distributed in the new modern democratic age where we have rule of the people, by the people for the people. It seems that the emperors may not have gone away. They have perhaps just changed their style and address, according to a report in the Guardian.

The extent to which so much global wealth has become corralled by a virtual handful of the so-called 'global elite' is exposed in a recent report from Oxfam [1]. It warned that some richest 85 people across the globe share a combined wealth of £1tn, as much as the poorest 3.5 billion of the world's population. These rich are in numbers a tenth of the one percent of the one percent of the one percent. Considering this fact, it is not surprising that much of whatever else that is left after the rich 85, is owned by far less than one percent of the population of the world, leaving the vast majority of around seven billion humans to struggle with the bills and in many cases with even the means to pay for their daily bread. In the new modern economy it does appear that nothing is going to trickle down, because it seems that it is not a trickle down economy anymore, it is a trickle up economy, except for the scraps a billionaire may throw around to advertise boldly in the media that he is in fact a philanthropist. You would rarely hear of the deeds of a real philanthropist because even their left hand may not know what the right is doing. A few of the latter kind are still around fortunately and make the world go on otherwise it may have been time for the Lord to call it quits as regards our planet.

It is a trickle up economy now. If it was not so, this kind of wealth inequality is a logical impossibility. A few pennies and dollars must be extracted from the hands and mouths of billions to build up such wealth, every hungry child and every desperate mother in the world, every clenched fist soaked with tears of desperation, even from the pockets of the infant sobbing besides his unconscious mother.

Presently in Syria the government gets the guns from Russia and the rebels from the rest of the world it seems. A long time ago General Eisenhower had said,

"Every single gun that is made, every warship launched, every rocket fired, signifies in the final sense a theft from those who hunger and are not fed, those who are cold and not clothed."

A Brief Introduction

The wealth accumulation is built up in the final sense, using General Eisenhower's words, by pulling out morsels from millions and billions of hungry mouths, from every pocket and every hand, even from naked tribes struggling to cover their shame and from the pockets of those with tear drenched eyes struggling to find the daily bread for a crying infant, from every family kicked out on homeless street during the last extraction by a gambler on wall street or the last shooting spree in Syria, Iraq, Sudan or Gaza.

Wealth pours in through multiple streams with the guns being just one, through various indirect means, some described later in this book (through methods such as inflation that amounts to stealing from the poor for the rich)

Is this surprising in a world where your elected representatives chosen by you, allow corporate honchos and bankers to walk away with millions in bonuses with a sweet rates of taxation and permit them to become too big to fail so that they can be bailed out with your money; or let old festering wars between nations and within nations continue through provocative measures and UN vetoes for decades rather than impose peace; how else can those lovely mansions by the waterside be procured? You, I and thousands of sweet little children of the world that struggle, even die daily of hunger; or war, are not important in this heady game.

The few have acquired their powers and wealth through wars from the beginning of human civilization and continue to do so even now in the so called democratic age. The only ray of hope is the open communication that has become available on the internet but its effect will take generations - old habits die hard. We deserve to be taken for a ride seeing that we are going to vote the same lot in again, and just in case a bank is fined millions for wrong doing as the RBS was in UK, it will be when it does not matter much to bankers who have already left with their handsome severance packages for their mansions in the Bahamas and other exotic locations. You shall help pay the fine because the bank shall be owned by the public because of the bailout as those in UK discovered.

A banker might chip in to add, a robber is such a fool to rob a bank with a gun when it is so easy and so very neat and legal to do it with a bonus. It is only the stupid who break a law, the clever make it. You may clarify that it is not the bankers and corporate owners who make laws but think about that again. Do you think it is a just law, dear reader, if it has allowed a handful of humans perhaps charged with insane greed or something far more sinister to control most of the world's wealth, over the tears, hunger and misery of billions of others? But then who ever said that Satan, even if he is symbol of something, and his Generals were not supposed to be sinister. Infants do not quench their thirst with water alone. There are tears too. Man does not live by bread alone. There is cake too. Since it is useless to criticize without suggesting solutions, this booklet shall suggest two very simple laws that if instituted will reduce poverty and inequality automatically and easily in any country while retaining capitalism with all its advantages but eliminating some of its biggest sins. They are known as the rule of ten and the rule of ninety respectively

An Online Reference

1. http://www.theguardian.com/business/2014/jan/20/oxfam-85-richest-people-half-of-the-world

Economics of Greed and Exploitation

2
When to Tax the Rich and when not to

There was a time when some humans developed the notion that all humans are created equal and that it is unjust for some to amass huge amounts of wealth while others grind their butts out. This notion gave birth to the idea of communism. However, the communists forgot that trees in a nearby forest are not all of equal height and that many humans are inherently lazy. Sans incentives and the need to grind their butts out, many humans would rather sit and fatten that area of their anatomy. The result was that bread lines became longer and longer until they became longer than the communist manifesto. The idea was therefore soon discarded into the trash can. Some political parties still call themselves communist but that is simply out of nostalgia. They neither mean it nor live by the philosophy any longer.

Capitalism thus marched across the world gloriously with the fond notion that if some individuals are allowed to grow exceptionally rich, it is good for business, and eventually prosperity for all would trickle down, bit by bit, as water does from a leaky jug. This gave birth to the notion of trickle down capitalism.

But, alas, humans, at least those blinded by greed, can be extremely exploitative, given the opportunity. Some have now invented a trickle up version of capitalism. They have invented systems so that it is not the case of water leaking down a jug but rather a case of a vampire sucking up the blood of the poor until they are snuffed out on homeless-street.

The ownership of substantial wealth has a certain psychological attempt on the owner. Not realizing that his ability has less to do with that state, and a set of fortunate circumstances more to do with it, many develop a swollen head thinking they are special. Further arises the need to protect what they have attained and they may even use unethical means or false arguments to perpetuate economic practices that ensure the wealth does not diminish. Rather, greed is insatiable. The more they get the more they want and with the means at their disposal they continue to invent newer practices for an extraction of yet more wealth from society until society ends up with a trickle up economy...

How does one distinguish a trickle down version of capitalism from a trickle up version? It is not all that difficult, if the average income of top one percent or ten percent (depending on choice of criterion) of population is rising while that of the bottom one or ten percent falls in real terms (adjusted for inflation) then it is a case of a trickle up economy. It happens when the income of those at the top keeps rising while average incomes do not. How can a trickle up economy come about? It is quite simple really when the taxation system, salary structure and printing of currency are in the hands of a few. It happens when share holders of a company have little say in deciding the pay packages of senior executives or when they have little say in how a public representative behaves soon after he is elected to office.

How does one know if a government is printing more money than necessary? Well, is there inflation of more than one or two percent around in your area? If it is then be sure that is what is happening although the guy controller up there called it something exotic like quantitative easing; and if a free floating currency is devaluing with respect to other countries.

Taxation: Whenever the issue of raising taxes on rich is considered in any country, arguments emerge that are for and against it. The fact of the matter is that there are times and countries where it is a good idea to do it as well as times and countries where it is detrimental. How does one determine which is which?

In order to ascertain if increasing or decreasing taxes of rich is called for, one needs to understand the trickle-up and trickle-down phenomenon. If it is found that the average income of top five percent in society has been increasing or decreasing over the past seven years (a reasonable time period to rule out temporary fluctuations) at the same rate as the overall average income in society, then the tax structures need not be changed. In case the income of top earners is falling at a faster rate than the average then a reduction in taxes of the rich may be called for rather than an increase. However, in case the income of top earners is rising at a rate that is faster than average income then an increase in taxes of the rich seems just, appropriate and useful for overall economic stability of a nation and to restore a fairer distribution of wealth.

Welfare: Welfare measures including subsidies that help the poor are directed at the bottom earners of society, the bottom ten percent or at least the bottom five percent such as creation of shelters for the homeless. Here too, whenever the question of increasing welfare spending in any country is considered arguments emerge for and against it. Increasing such spending could cause an increase of debt or fiscal deficits and thus hurt the economy in both the short and long term. In order to understand when increasing or decreasing welfare spending is called for, one need only look at change of income of the bottom five percent over the past few years and compare it to change in average income across the entire spectrum over the same period. In case income of the poor (adjusted for inflation of goods that matter to the poor such as food) is decreasing at a rate faster than overall average there is a desperate need to increase welfare spending. However, if income of the poor is increasing then perhaps a decrease in welfare spending may be considered. Such imbalances occur in an economy not because the poor are getting stupider and rich cleverer but simply because economic practices have become more exploitative and it is up to the governing structures to restore balance, to prevent it in the first place if possible and if they fail in that to do it with appropriate taxes.

If the income of poorer sections of society has been reducing over the past years while that of richer sections rising, this could be because of one of two reasons. Either the poor are becoming stupider and lazier than before while the rich cleverer and more hardworking or, the system is becoming more exploitative of the poor. It does not require more than common sense to realize that the reason for this imbalance can only be the latter. The exploitation and imbalance needs to be addressed on an urgent basis because whereas it may mean choice of home furnishing or size of the home for the rich, it implies the very life and death of poor and their children who are just as sweet as children of others or the choice of which homeless street to sleep on. The quickest way to address this imbalance and injustice is to increase taxes on richer sections of society and then using this revenue to assist the poor.

The world does not need communism but it does need justice and a move away from unfair inequalities, because it is the latter that has led to such extreme responses through human history as communism or severing the head of the queen from her torso when she suggested that people could eat cake when they ran out of bread.

The difference between working towards one's self interest and greed are as clear as the differences between eating a meal for living or gluttony or even the difference between an enjoyable sexual intercourse and gruesome rape, especially when it involves immoral behavior such as exploiting the vulnerable. Both self-interest and greed are qualitative phenomenon as indeed all emotional experiences are but rational humans can distinguish easily which is which. Those who try to confuse between the two are merely trying to rationalize or hide their shame and guilt that greed provokes in the ensuing confusion. Whereas working for ones living leads to well being, greed leads to misery just as gluttony does. When practiced on a wide scale in a nation, it leads to a collapse of national economies.

> The Economic debate of the time is no longer between communism and capitalism, left and the right, liberals or conservatives. It is about love and compassion, justice and fairness.

3

Inflation is like stealing from the Poor

In today's complex economy it is useful for ordinary citizens to understand a few simple principles about economics. That way, they can manage their own money better and also contribute their voice to policy making in their countries. This chapter is about inflation, its causes and ramifications and how it can be managed easily in any country.

Money is a used for acquiring goods and services and when the price of goods and services rise we say that inflation is taking place. The price of something depends on many factors but two of the primary ones are

1. Demand and supply balance

2. Extent of Money Supply.

Both factors are easy to understand. If a commodity becomes in short supply then its price tends to rise. If apple crops have been destroyed by untimely frost then apple prices will rise. If demand for a product increases then too its price rises but if demand decreases prices fall or crash. The balance of demand and supply is one of the factors that determine the price of any of the available goods or services.

Now let us understand money supply. For example, let us say any one country doubles its money printing and then distributes it by say doubling salaries. The price of everything in the country will tend to double because twice the money will be available for acquiring the same amount of goods and services. There was a time when governments could not print money at their own sweet will. It was when money was minted in gold and silver, but the world went off the gold standard a long time ago and that is no longer an impediment to printing more money if the policy makers so decide and the constitution permit it. Paper is cheaply available. Nowadays even paper is not required. All one has to do is punch some digits into a computer. However, even now, some countries cannot print their own money such as those in the Euro-zone; otherwise, Greece would have done it long ago to overcome its debt burden.

What would have happened if Greece had printed a lot of money? There would be inflation but the pensioners would not have been able to object as readily as they do now when their pensions are being reduced. They would get the same pension but it would buy less because of inflation and the effect would be the same. Any debt that Greece had in its own currency would be paid back easily and the creditors would not be able to complain because no one says that more has to be paid back if prices rise.

However, the portion of debt in dollars would increase because with inflation the price of dollar as determined by a flexible exchange rate would also rise. In this respect, USA is sitting pretty with its debt because most of its debt is in dollars and if that country prints a lot of extra money to cover it, it will pay it back easily, However that would also cause severe inflation with all the extra dollars floating around. Governments have nice names for printing excess money, perhaps so that people do not catch on. They have given it names like quantitative easing, debt or deficit monetization etc.

The Americans may have read this as a blog note because ever since it was public they have begun to do that in instalments. Their economy is being helped as a result and they may continue to do it until inflation becomes troublesome as it has as regards food.

Governments get their money through various sources like taxes, selling state assets, debt etc. They draw up a budget to spend this money. In case they spend more than their incomes, we have what is called a budget deficit. The deficit can easily be made up through quantitative easing i.e. printing more money and increasing money supply with the attendant consequence of inflation. In case, too much inflation takes place then controlling central banks tend to reduce money supply by various means such as increasing interest rates. The easiest way to curb inflation is to slash deficit budgets and increase interest rates until inflation is banished. In many developing countries the cause behind budget deficits is corruption because available money for budget is illegally misappropriated.

Whenever a question of reducing state budgets and deficits is considered, some economists immediately propose a reduction of subsidies that may be built into the system. Although certain subsidies may be undesirable, the worst time to reduce them is when inflation is already prevailing. It will simply increase inflation further for the most vulnerable sections of the country because the subsidies were introduced in the first palace because of such needs. It will particularly hit the population hurting from inflation most, increasing their misery. One may wonder why economists suggest such solutions to politicians for their approval even though it may lead to less than humanitarian consequence. The reason could be because it is not the economists who have to win votes. Their emoluments and compensation is best protected if there is GDP growth in the economy and that is best ensured through quantitative easing, no matter if the bottom half or even 99 per cent of the population suffers. The proper way to reduce deficits in inflationary times is to cut down non-subsidy expenditure such as Europe imposed on Ireland and Greece. It brings down inflation quickly and when that is banished, a government may consider reducing undesirable subsidies.

Some economists view inflation as a clever form of tax that gets money into the hands of governments cleverly without having to announce a tax increase. In the view of this blogger, if so, it is the most despicable form of tax because it taxes the poorest of the population, unlike Obama, who is trying to increase taxes for the richest Americans only who can easily afford it - persons making more than a quarter of a million a year. He is being given a hard time in the US congress because of it. Just shows how shameless some of the richest persons can be in protecting and increasing their wealth, aside from some exceptions like Warren Buffet.

What about inflation caused by a demand and supply imbalance? Will inflation not take place even without increased money supply if some item is in short supply? In this case the price of that item will increase for sure but then price of some other items will decrease if money in circulation remains the same and the overall rate of inflation across the board would not rise. Demand and supply imbalances and rise in price of imported things, tends to increase the price of specific items but do not cause general inflation across the board.

If financial practices are designed within a country so that inflation is intentional, it is an unfair practice of governance that is also inhuman because it hurts the poorer sections of society most. It is not any different to stealing from citizens, even the poor. If inflation within a country is not intentional but takes place inadvertently, it is a clear proof of mismanagement by government.

Ever since currency systems went off tangible things like gold or silver, it has become the responsibility of governments to manage production and distribution of their chosen currencies in a manner so that inflation or deflation does not take place except within a narrow band of one or two percent. Europe, Australia and USA have been efficient at such management, but not countries of Latin America, Africa and Asia.

The reasons for economies or individual price of goods going up or down are complex and include vagaries of nature and even psychology. Governments cannot be held responsible for it all. **However, the production and distribution of money is the responsibility of government and they are supposed to do it in a manner so that overall inflation (or deflation as in Japan) does not take place**. If they cannot, they have shirked their responsibility. If a nation is incompetent to do so, it should revert to the gold standard. Countries that have deflation like Japan are fortunate because they can easily get out of any recession by increasing money supply that is an easy process of printing money and in this special case it will be justified.

If one were to devise a *very rough thumb rule* for ascertaining the irresponsibility or immorality of government based on the rate of inflation then one might say approximately that a government is irresponsible to the extent of ten times the rate of inflation as a percentage of expected responsibility level. Thus a one per cent inflation rate may imply a ten per cent irresponsibility of government managed financial systems. Ten per cent inflation therefore may indicate one hundred per cent irresponsibility (unless it is a short term temporary blip). If it is still larger then the economic and financial system as well as the governance system that controls may be collapsed, malfunctioning or dishonest. If such a collapse is not due to something as severe as a war, then those who managed the financial system must be regarded as working against the interests of the people. The thumb rule here is highly approximate, as a first attempt, but the message is clear. In future better ones along the same lines may emerge that include a few other indicators such as exchange rate changes. A depreciation of currency is its effective devaluation and an indication that far more money is in circulation than warranted by the economic fundamentals.

At the present time, many countries are facing recession or slowing growth. One of the methods economists suggest and use to increase growth is to increase money supply. It may also increase inflation, but then, if the technique leads to an increase of income for all the citizens, they get compensated for increases in prices.

The present world economy has become such that even when growth takes place along with inflation then all citizens do not benefit equally. Unfortunately it is the rich who are benefiting most over the last decade and more as revealed by an increasing rich/poor ratios and the increasing ratio of the rich/poor incomes in most countries. In this scenario, the rich get compensated for any inflation that may be taking place whereas the effective income of the poor falls because of increased prices. **In effect, such a monetary easing results in taking money out of the pocket of the poor and transferring it to the pocket of the rich. It is happening now in many countries that are suffering inflation. It is in effect stealing from the poor for the rich.** Robin Hood is probably turning in his grave in Sherwood Forest because of this. He stole from the rich to give to the poor unlike some modern financial planners who are in effect doing the reverse while giving it fancy names like easing and covering it with intellectual sounding yet false arguments. There could be something noble about stealing from the rich, especially riches acquired unfairly and giving it to the poor. Wonder what the reverse is? You might try and make up a name for it even four letter ones perhaps.

In India where this author now lives, presently because of falling growth rate, industrialists are crying for a reduction of interest rates by the controlling bank so that growth rates are increased. **They are barking up the wrong tree though**. Interests are high because inflation is high and inflation is high because there is too much money in circulation because of fiscal deficits. They should be crying out for a reduction of fiscal deficits especially any part of it that is being monetized and not made up by debt. That will eventually automatically lead to the controlling bank reducing interest rates when inflation falls. The interest rates should in fact be higher because high inflation can lead to a near disaster of the financial system.

The author is presently very concerned about the greed of the grabbers that is pushing large sections of world population into financially difficult situations, hence the reason for writing this brief book.

This author is pleased to note that perhaps as a result of the principles explained in this note and mention of Japan in the original blog article, Japan began to pump money into its system and managed to get out of its decades long recession. The Prime Minister's party recently received a thumping victory. Best wishes to him. If he continues to follow it, the pumping of money should continue until inflation sets in, and best wishes to him also for restoring the lost historical national pride of Japan, that those who lose wars are made to do. Germany has already done it almost and it is high time Japan did it too. It is not that such simple principles are not known to economists of Japan, but knowledge is often held back due to vested interests. It gets implemented when made public.

4
The Rule of Ten

Recently there has been a hue and cry about high salary and bonuses that some corporate executives, especially bankers are drawing. The occupy movement that has erupted in many countries around the world represents this anguish of people. New sources of communication make expressing this anguish possible. There is a simple way to fix the problem. It is called the rule of ten here. If adopted such a rule will not only strengthen capitalism, it will also strengthen democracy. Simply stated this rule states that within any corporate or government organization the cumulative annual benefits (that include salary, bonuses, shares and all other benefits) of any individual within that organization shall not exceed ten times the total benefits of the lowest paid individual. This will immediately put a cap to the high bonuses and perks some individuals are enjoying in various organizations. The rule has to be corporation wide not country wide in order to allow corporations to compete.

The less severe version of this rule replaces the lowest salary in the above rule with average salary. However relating the highest wages to the lowest is the fairest practice.

The basis of this rule is that no individual is less than ten times as capable, hard working or talented than the most capable individual in any organization. In case he or she is, he/she should be in a care home instead. It is only just that the salary structures reflect this reality. Why ten and not nine or eleven? Well some number has to be chosen and a round number is simple to implement. However the Swiss has chosen the number as twelve after this blog post was circulated on the net in order to relate salary to the months in a year. Any number may be chosen as becomes acceptable for a start just as long as the salary of top executives are not allowed to run away until they hit the roof.

The real and evident reason for these gross inequalities is that those with advantages have exploited their positions to extract their pound of flesh since the dawn of human civilization. However, the base has got broader with time, from a single King or dictator to at least around one per cent. With further evolution the trend is bound to accelerate. This author too has belonged to the one per cent for most of his life, but if he speaks against it, it is because of his spiritual leanings that regard exploitation of humans by other humans as unfair.

Countries not used to this sort of rule will find it rather extreme, but they can make a beginning by a rule of 20, 30, 40 or 50 in its place to prevent a few individuals from ripping off the voiceless shareholder and the shirts off the back of the poor

How will such a rule strengthen democracy? If a referendum is to be called for such a law an overwhelming majority shall support it. Any rule or law that is in accordance with the just aspirations or wishes of the people and is workable strengthens democracy. What about the argument being put by some bankers etc. that this will lead to a flight of talent. That is just nonsense.

Such a rule will not lead to a flight of talent. It shall lead to a flight of greed and exploitation instead.

What will happen to the campaign contributions of political candidates if some individuals and corporations are not allowed to get disproportionately rich? No just human society needs campaign contributions that ride on the back of the homeless and the struggling while the likes of Mr. Gambler has perhaps taken off to their island spa for another bunga bunga party. Quite likely he has enough room for other leaders to join him as other economies around the world collapse under the burden of debt.

Unless the presently prosperous economies of the world take steps towards limiting high executive rip-offs and take care of national debt they are headed to certain economic doom. Current measures as being adopted around the world only kick the can down the road, a road on which the pits get deeper as one moves further.

A few years ago, when the CEO of a Swiss drug major was walking off with a seven million severance package, as approved by a board of directors whose compensations he had approved (it is the you scratch my back, I scratch yours story in corporations) the Swiss public woke up and forced in a new law to prevent this sort of rip offs by companies. The legislators cried foul and the companies cried foul but the public had their way because of the unique sort of democracy the Swiss have. In other countries the public does not have a similar say.

This post on the internet and its reprints elsewhere on the net have resulted in the Swiss 1:12 initiative that the Swiss attempted. Understandably there is much opposition to it from the same quarters that uphold the 1 per cent dominance in the world and it is possible that it may not win just right now but it is clear that the idea has arrived. Similar moves are underway in other nations too, albeit in their infancy just now. Read more about this here

Raising the Minimum Wage is a Poor Idea

Rather than using the wage ration rule here, often we hear talk of raising the minimum wage in different economies of the world. The people who ask for this are those who have got trapped into an exploitative economy where a few control most of the wealth and raise the minimum wage of the poor from time to time as feudal lords used to raise the salary of their servants and slaves from time to time. What need be addressed instead are income inequalities but those can be done by controlling the maximum wage not just the minimum one. Raising minimum wages could cause maximum wages to rise faster, increasing inequalities further and inflation could erode the value of minimum wage even if increased as has happened in many countries. One might say that raising minimum wage could reduce inequality but that is a poor way to go about it. There is a far better way that has something to do with a ratio as explained in the rule of ten. It is not an advanced concept. Elementary school children learn about it in arithmetic nowadays. Whenever minimum wages are raised but no caps of any form are put on the maximum wages it is mere appeasement and a travesty. It permits senior executives to take away a huge chunk of profits as salary, bonuses and various other benefits, profits that would have been shared with the shareholders and all employees or used to expand and strengthen the business. When the business fails the public may pay again for the bail out perhaps. The UK public paid a third time for one of the bailed banks when it was fined millions for wrong doings. It was the bank that paid the fine but the bank was with the public by now so it was the public paying the fines. Those who had committed the wrongs were relaxing in their mansions with the help of millions in severances packages they took when they left.

Fixing a minimum wage is most detrimental to a new small business or even a large struggling one. It can lead to collapse of the business as it does from time to time and everyone ends up losing then. Better have a low wage then end up on the street without a job. If the economy or a business organization improves all would be helped and the minimum wage would automatically go up provided one understands how to use something called a ratio. When ratios are fixed senior executives have to raise the minimum salaries in an organization if they want their own salaries increased.

It is not suggested that incomes of all should be equal as some communists did. That kills incentive to work and even the trees in a forest are not all of equal size. Some inequality is natural but it is not natural to have a million feet high tree in the forest either. Rather, what is suggested is that there must be some reasonable ratio of the maximum and minimum wages within each organization say ten, twenty or thirty times at the most. This will permit small businesses to grow starting with a low wage for everyone from cleaner to CEO and also permit struggling industries to survive through lean periods by cutting benefits of all across the board. It would also prevent greedy bankers from running away with the profits or gambling too much with other people's money in the hope of a bonus. Such a proposal under the name of rule of ten was proposed by this author a few years ago and has been enthusiastically examined by many Europeans.

The reason why some forms of communism failed is because it was sought to impose an unnatural equality on the masses. The reason why many forms of capitalism are struggling and reeling under debt, stress and homelessness is because an unnatural inequality has been permitted to flourish. The solution is the middle road. If they can walk it in

Sweden while merrily singing the song of prosperity so can the others because Sweden is not a planet in a galaxy far far way.

5
Proportional Tax – A New Method of Corporate Taxation

A new method of corporate taxation termed proportional tax is described. It is simpler than existing methods of taxation yet it appears to be powerful in implementing economic policy and directing corporate behavior in desirable directions. Proportional tax for corporations is different from proportional tax for individuals. While proportional tax for individual implies that they pay the same proportion of income as their tax, whatever is their level of income, for corporations it implies here that they pay tax at a rate that is proportional to their net profit. This chapter contains some simple mathematical points and those not interested in that may safely skip to the next chapter without any substantial loss.

Introduction:

While communism appears to have failed in most countries, capitalism has been more successful in meeting human needs and improving the quality of life of humans. However, it has not been an unblemished victory for capitalism. Problems have occurred because of an excess of greed or because of use of unethical practices to satisfy that greed. It may be pointed out that unethical practices are frequently more insidious than illegal ones. Illegal practices can be dealt with by law but it is impossible to deal with unethical practices until new laws are created to cover them. The huge compensations, bonuses and severance packages that senior executives of some corporation draw fall in the realm of unethical practices. It has led to the financial crisis of 2008. Unfettered greed of corporations have also led to rising inequalities that have forced some to homelessness while the wealth of the world has been captured by fewer and fewer individuals.

Various mixed models that combine elements of both, communism with capitalism, have also been attempted in parts of the world. Some of these have failed such as those employed in the period between 1950 and 1990 in India while some have done fairly well as in Scandinavian countries.

Whereas communism depends upon the state to provide goods and services, capitalism depends upon individual initiative to meet the same needs. Except for minor goods and services on a small scale that can be produced by an individual or an individual family most goods and services require that humans get together to create organizations for the purpose. Such organizations as legal entities are corporations and they are the main stay of a capitalistic economy.

It has been recognized that capitalism cannot function without regulation, for example preventing the development of monopolies that eliminate competition. If national economies have to continue with capitalism they must continuously evolve new practices, laws and regulations. It must be pointed out that whatever the economic model used, it is a tool to serve humans and wherever that purpose is defeated, resulting in inhumane consequences then economic activity degenerates into a tool for exploiting humans rather than serving them. While regulations control undesirable behavior of corporations, they also make life difficult for other corporations that may be behaving perfectly well. Thereby regulation also hampers economic activity. Therefore, in designing regulations care must be exercised towards simplicity and ease of application of the regulatory regime. In the present connected world, it is a wise course to study best practices of other countries and adapt these to suit one's needs rather than inventing new practices that may turn out to be unsuccessful in the long run. However, this does not mean that new regulations need not be explored. Human innovation is an ongoing process just as human evolution is. It is with this in view that a new way of implementing corporate taxes is introduced briefly in this note. The simplicity of this new idea is such that it neither requires a lengthy explanation nor support by several other studies and references.

The new method termed Proportional Tax is simple to apply; in fact it is simpler than existing methods that have graduated discrete slabs. Aside from being a way to tax, the new proposal may also be used as powerful tool to discourage some of the worst practices of capitalism while encouraging the best ones. This new method was born out of a somewhat informal note by this author elsewhere called the 'Rule of Ninety' and it may also be referred with this latter name. It may be pointed out that the new proportional tax is specific for corporate taxes. Analogous methods do not apply to individual taxes.

Corporate taxes

Most countries impose corporate tax, also called corporation tax or company tax. Generally corporate taxes are charged as a percentage of net profits after allowing for certain deductions. Rates may vary between ten and fifty percent in most cases. While corporate taxes are an important source of revenue they are also used as policy measures, for example, exempting a certain industry such as the renewable industry from taxes or charging a graduated rate of tax to encourage new small businesses. However, existing methods of taxation are a limited tool in implementing policy. For example, they cannot prevent development of huge corporate monopolies on their own nor can they prevent excess profiteering. The new method called proportional tax can do all that existing methodologies of corporate taxation do, while doing much more to control corporate behavior in desirable directions in a straight forward and simple manner.

New Proportional Tax:

Proportional Tax implies that rate of corporate tax is proportional to net profits, NP, in a continuous manner rather than in discrete slabs. A constant of proportionality is required to determine the tax rate. Aside from the proportionality constant the new method may also prescribe a minimum threshold rate of corporate tax to prevent near zero rates of taxation for companies making small profits. It will be shown that this simple method has powerful mathematical properties that make it a powerful tool in the hands of policy makers and the public.

Consider,

Rate of Corporate Tax = 100 (Net Profits/M)

The constant of proportionality, M, here is shown as an inverse constant in order to give it a physical meaning. M may be visualized as the net profit of a reference virtual mega corporation that has a very large profit, larger than the expected profit of any other corporations in the country. Thus if a company makes one fourth the amount of net profit as M then its corporate tax rate shall be 25 percent as per the given formula.

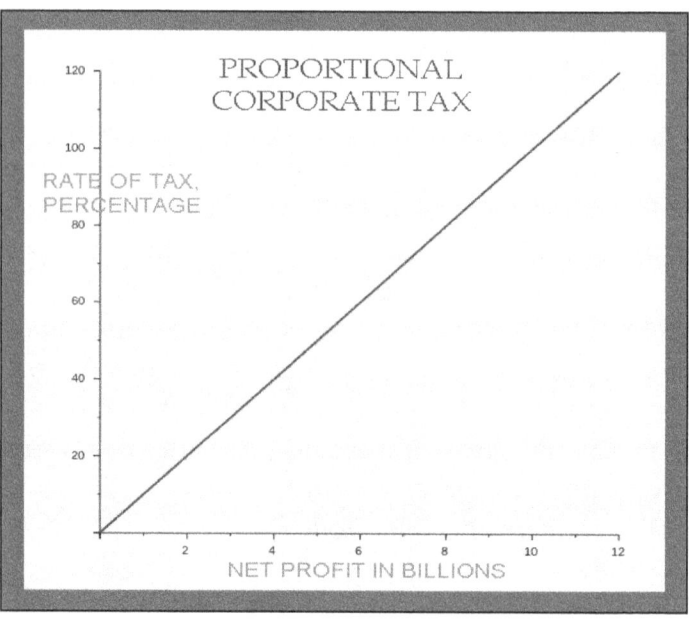

Figure 1 Corporate Tax rates as proportional to net profits

Figure 1 illustrates how corporate tax rates vary with net profits in billions of dollars. In this illustration, M has been selected as ten billion dollars. If a minimum threshold tax, T is selected as 20 percent and if M has been chosen at the outset as a suitably high number e.g. two and a half times the maximum net profit of any company, then tax rates for all companies in this example shall vary within a narrow band of twenty and forty percent. Different rates of tax can be promulgated depending upon choice of M and T. The variation of rates is a simple linear one but its ultimate effect on corporations is far from linear as shown next.

Profits after Tax

Profit after Tax termed as P here as different from the net profit, NP before tax is

$$P = NP - NP \, (NP/M)$$

Figure 2 shows how residual profit after tax, P varies with net profit, NP, if M= 10 billion and T = 0. The unique feature of this variation is that beyond a certain level of net profits, residual profit of a company begins to fall and in extreme cases becomes negative. This very feature of the new proposal is a powerful controlling mechanism that may be used if a country wishes to reduce the size of certain corporations e.g. banks that might become too big to fail.

Figure 2 shows how residual profit after tax, P varies with net profit, NP, if M= 10 billion and T = 0. The unique feature of this variation is that beyond a certain level of net profits, residual profit of a company begins to fall and in extreme cases becomes negative. This very feature of the new proposal is a powerful controlling mechanism that may be used if a country wishes to reduce the size of certain corporations e.g. banks that might become too big to fail.

All companies would like to make the highest possible residual profits. However, they will be obliged not to charge such a high price for their products, even if they can, so that net profits increase beyond the point that their actual profit reduces or even results in a loss for the company.

Proportional tax as defined here for corporations is different from proportional tax for individuals. While proportional tax for individual implies that they pay the same proportion of income as their tax, whatever is the level of income, for corporations it implies here that they pay a tax at a rate that is proportional to net profit. The considerations and criterion that apply to individuals are very different to those that apply to corporations and therefore analogous methods of taxations do not apply.

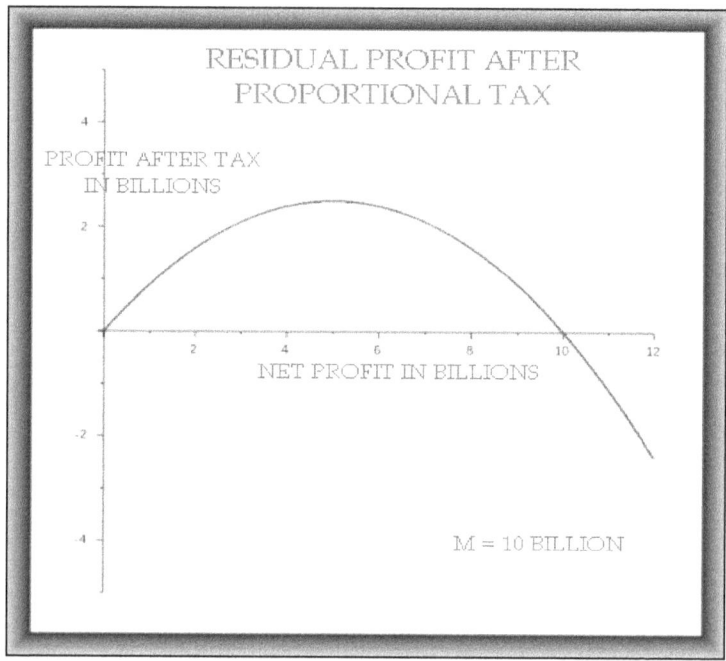

Figure 2 Residual Profits after Tax

Choice of constants M and T

Constants M and T can be chosen for the economy as a whole or they may chosen as different for different sectors of the economy. Thus if a country feels that a monopoly has developed in the automobile sector and other players need to be encouraged, it may set M as a value equal to the expected profit of the particular monopolistic automobile company. That company would then end up paying near hundred percent taxes while newer smaller players will be encouraged to develop with lower rates of taxes.

It must be noted that since tax rate depends on net profits, the single large automobile company can still keep new players out by bringing down its prices and reducing its net profit in order to maintain a high residual profit. But that is something that will benefit consumers. It is good corporate behavior in the interest of all. This type of monopoly needs to be encouraged rather than discouraged since it has become self regulated from within rather than from competition.

Maximizing Profits

In Mathematical theory we learn that there can be only one single goal that can be maximized or minimized in any operation and this single goal for corporations in capitalism and traditional economic theory has been to maximize profits. However, this goal is neither laudable nor sustainable and another far worthier goal is to maximize customer satisfaction. Because of this the focus of business has been on the bottom line. Spurred on by activist shareholders, private-equity firms, and bonuses based on stock prices, corporate managers have become obsessed with maximizing quarterly profits and while some profits hit an all-time high as a percent of the economy, the economy as a whole does not grow nor do jobs and real incomes of the majority. This obsession with profit maximization that has been supported by modern capitalistic theory is downright detestable if not evil. It is to glorify one of the biggest weaknesses of humans – greed.

One result of the profit obsession, for example, is that big companies pay the lowest possible wages and income inequalities tend to increase. The rule of ten is a handy tool to fix this evil quickly. The same can be said for big banks like Bank of America, Citigroup, and many other huge American companies that are engaged in finding ways to fire people and cut costs. In addition to their massively profitable Wall Street operations, these banks have huge branch networks in which tellers and local loan officers make modest salaries while serving their communities.

Profit maximization leads to a whole host of evils that have given capitalism a bad name that it can do without since really that is the only natural way for the needs of a society to be met .It results in countless inefficiencies such as multiple products being bought where one would do, unnecessary upgrades, deliberate damaging or even disposal of working products and restrictions on product use. The consequence of this is that customers and the environment both suffer. To fix this, companies need to change their prime goal from maximizing profit to maximizing customer satisfaction. Certainly this does not mean that the company should not make any profit. If that happens the company would not only be not able to grow but also collapse. However the profit has to be a secondary constraint not the prime goal. It would be in the long term interest of any company to do so. The question is how to make companies do that. In economics, profit maximization is the process by which a firm determines the price and output level that returns the greatest profit. The first place to start is for economists to stop regarding this as something glorious but as something shameful, a necessary encumbrance, even shameful. If one were to make a gross analogy the aim of a human should not be to maximize shit but well being, even though the shit is a necessary encumbrance that has to be tolerated. Profits may be viewed in the same manner. Profits can not be stopped though just as shit cannot or there would be a collapse.

Measures like the rule of ninety are a great and simple tool available to governments to force the largest companies away from the goal of maximizing profits, and becoming too big to fail or a monster that controls society.

Conclusion

A new way of applying corporate taxes called proportional tax is described. An appropriate choice of parameters, M and T, is required in the new method of proportional tax, for different sectors of the economy or the economy as a whole. The new method appears to be a powerful tool to manage corporate behavior so as to bring out its best its best while discouraging practices that are detrimental to society at large. It merits further study by economists and policy makers in order to explore its full implications before implementing as a new corporate taxation method, if desired.

Symbols used in this chapter

NP, Net Profit

P, Residual Net Profit after tax

M, An inverse constant of proportionality

T, Minimum threshold tax rate

Some Useful References

1. Steven A. Bank (2011). **Anglo-American Corporate Taxation: Tracing the Common Roots of Divergent Approaches**, Cambridge University Press.

2. The Corporate Income Tax System: Overview and Options for Reform, Mark P. Keightley and Molly F. Sherlock (2014), CRS Report for Congress, Prepared for Members and Committees of Congress. Online document

6
The Paradox of Modern Life and Economy

There was a time when a very substantial portion of human population lived off the land in rural areas scattered across the planet. Since the industrial revolution, large portions of human population began to move towards cities to engage themselves in industrial production and other pursuits related to an urban life. Consumption of energy and industrial production began to increase and with advent of things like antibiotics, human population too began to increase rapidly. Nations that could produce and consume at increasingly large rates or provide for increasing consumption to other parts of the world grew rapidly. It is here that an inherent paradox and contradiction began to be built into modern economies.

Many realize that current rates of consumption in the most developed economies such as the US are not sustainable. As resources like energy and materials diminish, the planet is running out of cheap resources. On the other hand if humans begin to reduce consumption and return to simpler lifestyles, the economies will stop growing and sink into recession. It is a case of die if you do and die if you don't. That is why economists in the US jump with glee when retail sales and consumption increases but that pushes up the cost of dwindling resources like fossil fuels and the economy tends to push back into recession all over again causing repeated dips.

Of the two scenarios, one of increasing consumption and the other of reduced consumption, common sense appears to suggest that reducing consumption, at least excesses and wastages, is the enlightened way to go. It should be welcomed. However, governments and economists would prefer that this does not happen because if consumption reduces, GDP growth reduces. The national budgets are a percentage of GDP. Therefore an economy in recession implies that governments would be compelled to either reduce expenditure or go into debt; or go into deficit and monetize the deficit (print more paper money in excess of GDP). But then a day comes when the debt becomes too large to service, some of it is defaulted and cheap debt is no longer available as has happened in Greece.

Incase a government reduces expenditure then it is unpopular with the population as is Greece, Ireland or UK currently. An unpopular democratic government then gets thrown out in a democratic election. In case the government goes into debt, it can postpone its problems for a future government or future date. If deficits are monetized then inflation takes place and that is like an additional tax on all citizens, an invisible tax that is not shown in tax returns but hurts much more since it hurts the poor as well. Since democratic countries are the dominant ones in the world today, hence an economic philosophy that is favored by governments that are elected for short terms prevails. Hail consumption! Who cares for grandchildren? The sad truth in some countries though is that they are the grandchildren of past excesses. The future is here.

In the meantime, while governments struggle with these problems, some people loose their jobs and end up on the street. A friend, John, commented in his blog that persons ending up on the street and begging are despised. To my mind stepping out of the economy and its stress is not such a bad idea for a person who is willing to enjoy not much more than sunshine and fresh air. However, if a person gets into begging that is despicable since it involves bumming on someone else. It is better for such persons to return to the land if they can and make a simple living out of it. Backed by the government a planned move back to the land can create a huge number of quality jobs and there are posts on that in my blog **http://someitemshave.blogspot.com** called AM farms that provides a rural alternative to urbanites with advantages of both town and country. Just search for it using a search tool if you are interested

I presently live in India (after having lived in other parts from Canada to the Middle East) and have witnessed the rural way of living that is still not very different in some parts to the way of living prior to the industrial revolution. In some cases the life is hard, especially if the weather gods have been unkind (The worst off were those that went into debt from time to time encouraged by modern or traditional bankers, eventually forced into suicide) but in other cases and that is still the majority, rural farmers have a little surplus to tide them over the bad years. They do not have the luxuries of modern societies but they are stress free and happier as a result of it, most times. If they have some surplus they build a cement and concrete house. If they do not have a surplus they build a mud and thatch house that comes for free. It requires labor but the labor is often spread across several years so that it is not a pain. They have no money for medical treatment and medical drugs. Hence they die peacefully without having to suffer debilitating side effects and conditions like cancer. Most are able to grow enough wheat for their own consumption and if you think carefully this is a versatile food grain, a variety of grass that can sustain a human diet. Think of the many forms wheat can be turned into. First there is a range of leavened and unleavened breads. Then we have cookies, biscuits and cake, with a bit of processing one may have noodles, pasta, pizza, khus khus (a North African thing) and a croissant. When one grows wheat then that produces fodder for the cows. Farmers who keep up to four cows end up with at least one that is in the milking stage and that provides butter and more protein or cheese. Once in a while two or three cows begin to produce milk simultaneously and that is the time to sell some milk and get a new wardrobe for the family. When a farmer gets too old to farm, either his son does the farming or he sells/rents his land and lives off that. No wonder more of poor rural persons laugh more often than rich urban ones who are found to be irritable and sulking frequently instead.

When I told a modern economist of an economic model based on reduced growth (that included proportionately reduced government expenditure) for a change, the urban economist laughed heartily. The laughter was a pleasant change. He remarked that a diet based on wheat is not a low carb diet that he is currently on. None of the farmers I met had ever heard of a low carb diet. When told about it they laughed heartily.

Economics of Greed and Exploitation

7
Fixing the Banks

It appears that before the financial crisis a few years ago the Royal bank of Scotland was indulging itself in risky investment gambling. It is a really fun game where bankers in nice white shirts and bright ties play on a computer screen for huge profits. Mind you there is no stress of risk. It is not their money they play the game with. They gamble with our money. They are smart and talented at the game and therefore win most times. The winnings are distributed under the name of a bonus that is on top of their already hefty salaries for coming in every day to the bank to play the game. If asked to leave the bank, they do not mind they have signed up for a hefty severance package before they joined.

But guess what, gambling is gambling and does involve the risk of losing. When they lost heavily before the financial crisis the poor fellows were consoled by their bosses by giving them a bonus anyway, albeit a slightly smaller one. The losses suffered by the bank as a whole were made up by the British Public. The government as a result has ended up with a bigger deficit that they are making up by cutting public programs leading to a loss of jobs for many. Any way, the homeless guy on the street or the poor wife who consoled her children that meat would be back on the table soon after papa finds a new job were consoled by the government that they were now owners of eighty percent or so of RBS, the royal bank of Scotland, and it was sure to help them in future.

It seems this year the bank profited at gambling again and the bankers are sharing a big chunk of the profits again. Some of them perhaps need to refurbish their holiday homes and yachts with new trappings. The old brocade ones get tiresome after a season or two. In the meantime the government has found that the bank was rigging something called Libor rate and has asked the British Public who own the bank, 600 million or so for the offence, No, no, bonuses or salaries of the banking executives will not be cut. How can they do a thing like that? Perhaps some of them can help encourage campaign contributions from industry for the elections and facilitate it by advancing loans to those industries. In any case what is the need for these smart bankers to suffer when we have the generous public to bail them out?

I am not a banker and perhaps I have figured out all this wrong, or anyone else who knows more about this fun game finds the time to oblige. While some of this is written in a satirical side after indignation at news about LIBOR fines, the remaining section is more serious.

Organizations are run by people and building good organizations requires honest, talented and dedicated workers who value their work and whose judgment is not impaired by baser human instincts such as lust, pride, greed etc. This is as true for banking industry as it is for any other industry. Creating a good banking structure and therefore also improving the economy by implication requires excellent talent. However, this statement needs to be understood properly with respect to the modern banking industry before it can be implemented.

The talent required for running banks is of two types. It is absolutely essential to understand these two types of talents. A confusion between the two is at the root of the present economic woes of many developed countries and therefore also the rest of the world.

The first is the straight forward traditional honest banking that requires specialized training, education and experience. There is really no dearth of financial services professionals possessing these skills, especially now with lay offs in the sector.

However, there is a second aspect to modern banking that involves risky investment banking and use of complex financial dealings. Talent in this latter area is severely limited. There are only a few professionals who can do this skillfully and profitably most of the time. There are other associated skills too, such as, lobbying with media and legislators, creating rationale for hefty compensations and bonuses, even rigging things like LIBOR rate while attempting to stay within the limits of law. These latter skills that some might even informally classify as wheeling and dealing or casino style banking with other people's money are severely limited in the industry. Persons possessing these latter skills perhaps head many modern banks and draw millions in compensation for their services from these banks.

In case a government of any country passes a legislation that limits total compensation (that includes salary, bonuses and any other benefits) of senior banking executives to say a quarter of million dollars a year or another specified by proposals of an earlier chapter, this latter talent and expertise in wheeling and dealing banking will fly away. They will go to other countries that are still paying millions in compensation. The banking industry of the country from which the talented wheeler dealers fly away will be left in the hand of traditional bankers. Their profitability will be restored since it will be left in the hands of the sincere straight forward bankers drawing handsome but not exorbitant benefits. The health of the banking industry of such a country would then be restored. By implication the economy of such a country will also get a boost since much depends on how banks operate. In short it will be good if the so called present banking talent flies away to other destinations and the quickest way to do it is limit their salaries and bonuses.

It is the simplest route to restoring banks and the first logical step to restoring economy; but are the persons who have the power to make such changes interested in giving up their present advantages?

A Brief Introduction

8
Future of World Economies – Green Thoughts

Developed economies of the world, reeling under debt and rising unemployment, have been facing severe economic pressures ever since a financial crisis began in 2008.

One may wonder as to where the future of developed economies is heading. The developed economies still lead the world in high technology manufacture such as such as computer chips, aircraft etc. They will probably continue to do so for several more decades. However for the rest of manufacturing, ranging from undergarments to motorcars, it appears that high standards of living coupled with high wages in developed countries makes much of manufacturing uncompetitive in a globally trading world. It is partly for this reason that economies of the BRIC countries are growing rapidly while developed economies stagnate or struggle with insignificant growth.

The largest of developed economies, the US that is largely consumer driven hopes to grow once again if consumer demand increases. However a sustainable future for mankind does not lie in increasing consumption but rather reducing consumption if it is already excessive and far above world averages. This is even more valid in a world where basic resources such as fossil fuels are rapidly being exhausted and consequently becoming more expensive with time. It is true that other sources of energy such as wind and solar will eventually replace traditional sources of energy but they are unlikely to be as cheap as fossil fuels prepared for free by Mother Earth. Developed economies like USA must also consider that if consumption and retail sales do begin to rise again this may not be a win-win situation if increased demand is catered to by trade deficits. Indeed that is what is likely to happen.

The other route suggested by economists of old is of stimulating growth through large government spending. This too appears to be a losing game in the present scenario if spending leads to more debt by governments already overburdened by debt. In future, it is becoming increasingly clear that democratic governments would have to be obliged to live within their means. However in the meantime debt exists and one has to live and deal with it and the accompanying pain. Large stimuli are provided in the hope that they will eventually lead to rising demand and restore economy on a path of growth fuelled by ever rising consumption. However this may not happen anymore and one may find that after the stimulus is exhausted the economy sinks once again. Indeed some such thing may have already happened with the earlier trillion-dollar stimulus of the American economy.

There exist some basic danger points in western economies that can trigger a recession once again any time in the future. Indeed the Present Governor of the Reserve Bank of India – Raghuram Rajan – who had predicted the financial crisis of 2008 thinks so. One is government debt that has already been mentioned. Future generations must learn the lesson now and prevent governments from undertaking that route again. It is likely that they would have to add such safeguards into their constitutions because democratic government decisions are partly based on winning the next election. If such short-term goals are partly met by incurring a debt, left for the future generations to pay, then a time may come that the future debt becomes much too large to handle. Indeed it has already happened in most developed economies, most obviously in Greece, and a little less obviously yet in other developed countries. Greece has led the western civilization for two and half millennia followed by Rome and perhaps it is symbolic that they should lead the decline too.

A second danger point, that was the trigger for the most recent economic recession, is the behavior of private corporations such as banks. The total emoluments of the highest paid executives of such banks comprising of salary, bonus perks and benefits are such that they are several times the emoluments of the lowest paid employees of the same organization. The justification for that is that if these corporations make huge profits, the senior executives deserve a share. Does it have anything to do with greed? Senior executives need to eat better perhaps! A second rationale is that if they did not do it, a flight of talent will take place. Both these arguments are suspect. First if a corporation makes a huge profit then all its employees are responsible and not just the chief. What is the justification for the salary being one hundred times or more? Is ten or even twenty times not enough?

What if there was a law in a country that dictated that the highest emolument of any employees might not be more than ten or twenty times that of the lowest paid employee? In that case, the senior management of the organization in direct or indirect collusion with the board members (The Goldman Sachs directors for example draw millions in compensation) would not be able to draw such high salaries, bonuses and perks. The profits would then have to be shared equitably with all employees or shareholders instead. Therefore such a law is indeed fair and worth considering. What about the flight of talent? That is so much baloney to the mind of this author. There are hundreds of others, even some unemployed that are more talented than the CEO's of many such high paying corporations. Placed in that position they would perform just as well. No human is hundred times more talented than other humans unless that other human is an idiot.

A senior executive is given a large bonus if his company makes a large profit. The situation becomes insidious if the large profit is made by gambling as in investment banking. Larger the risk, larger the profits!

Gambling is legal in many countries. Gambling with other people's money appears to be legal in banks. If a large profit is made, the Board and the executives pocket the bonus. If it results in loss, the bank has still enough reserves for them to draw a smaller bonus and move on. If the bank crashes the directors and chief executives do not mind. They have already made their money and need time off to enjoy it now. The investors and shareholders can stay back to drown in their tears.

Governments complained about this practice soon after the recession in 2008 and a little after pushed the matter under the carpet. The only government that has taken some steps in trying to insulate the public from the potential loss appears to be the UK government. They have developed a plan to implement albeit after a decade or so – long after the Greek and other crisis have eaten some more banks and the savings and pension funds of more of the public. The risk continues and if recession and unemployment was not sufficient for governments to act, perhaps they never will, at least not in our generation.

Returning back to our speculation on the future of developed or western economies it can be appreciated that the situation is somewhat different in the old and the new world. Countries like USA, Australia and Canada have huge land resources and fresh water sources as compared to the old world. A possibility is that future Jobs in countries like USA would come from small-scale intensive agriculture. This intensive agriculture consists of small farms of about ten acre sizes that involve labor intensive agriculture practices such as diary, horticulture, poultry, cheese making etc. With an increasing population around the world, there is a world demand for food. Thus, whereas countries like china or India can produce underwear or even a motorcar cheaply they are unable to produce enough food to control food prices within their countries in a rising demand scenario. Certainly this sort of future growth would involve a major shift in attitudes and practices in a country like USA, but it appears to be a feasible path. Such a solution however may not be available to Europe and Japan where land resources are limited and whatever exists is already being used intensively. Perhaps then a cycle of history will repeat that swept from Greece to Rome to Europe and the New World over a period of two and a half millennia.

9
A Spiritual view of the Economy

At various places in spiritual forums this author mentioned his belief in reincarnation. A question that was asked in such discussions was – if humans are a result of reincarnation, how has the population of humans increased so drastically. There can be more than one source for that increase. First is the reduction of animals and insects on the planet that has taken place simultaneously. Another source is other similar planets. A third is souls that may have been waiting without bodies to be born at the right time.

The state of humans really does vary from animal like to god-like on earth. The greatest variation can be seen in countries like India rather than a largely tribal African country or a well developed European one. At one time I use to be saddened and agitated at the near animal like behavior of some humans and human habitations. Many rural Indians still live in homes without a loo, using open spaces to do the necessary job, and this when private bathrooms were common in the same country some four thousand years ago(Indus Valley civilization). It does not cost much to build a toilet and septic tank, provided one cared to. However I have reconciled to the sad state. This does not imply that one should not help others improve whenever an opportunity arises to do so. However this may be done in small steps only without much expectation. As regards what one might teach a human who lives poorly if the opportunity arose – it seems best to teach them the same sort of things as one would others who may be considered as highly evolved beings – shun violence, greed, lies etc. in all its forms. However the most learning has to be directed inwards to one's own self. There is something of an animal in all of us. Less developed souls may take to physical violence readily but other humans who have rejected that mode of behavior also resort to it at the level of speech and thought. To my mind a god-like human i.e. one who is ready to step out of human life into the next higher life form in the universe is one who has overcome jealousy, anger, greed and lust.

When I mention overcoming lust I do not imply overcoming sexual interests that are subservient to romantic love or a part of it but sexual interests that are devoid of it i.e. purely physical. A far more common problem with humans is that of greed, and that too must be overcome before human attention can be directed to higher pursuits. Much human happiness lies elsewhere – in health, love, peace, freedom etc. that do not require money to acquire. In the ultimate analysis, humans need relatively little money for their most essential of material needs of food and shelter. True there are very many on earth deprived even of that. The problem is, as soon as a human is able to achieve the goal of basics, he wants even more, so that usually it the most well off who appear to be the most greedy.

My mind goes to rich corporate executives especially those in the banking industry with salaries in millions of dollars a month who appeared to be agitated by an order of the US President Obama limiting the salary to half a million soon after the financial crisis, if they belonged to an organization that was being assisted by public money. Opponents to the move said that this will lead to a loss of talent. To my mind any human who is greedy enough to be unsatisfied with a salary of half a million dollars (plus perks) cannot be mature or talented but rather someone who will lead an economy into still greater distress. Such a person can not be mature enough to manage our money. He may have been mature at one time, but not any more. Greed blinds a human just as lust and anger does, rendering the wisest as imbeciles. All of us surely know instances of that from our own lives. The tragedy is that although there are safety valves to lust and anger that put a stop to it sooner rather than later there are no such safety valves to greed. Once it enters a psyche it takes an indefinitely long time to leave.

In the ultimate analysis it is the cumulative effect of greed that has lead to the current economic down turn. This greed has not just been the greed of ordinary citizens but also that of persons at the helm in governments and private corporations. Over the past half century greed appears to have grown faster than the economy in the most prosperous countries around the world. True to human nature - the greater the growth, the greater the increase of greed. The recession will end durably only when this greed has been knocked down to manageable levels, not before. There is no economic plan or stimulus that can restore prosperity that does not address the issue of human nature that eventually dictates how prosperous a nation is.

If a collapse is held back by a national bail out and debt the can with the bomb be kicked down the road to some date in future but with the attendant problem that the explosive force would be larger whenever it happens.

Ancient literature has described greed as one of the three qualities that leads a human to hell, the other two being lust and anger. Plato's moral argument against greed is that individual greed benefits one person at the expense of others; systemic greed can damage an entire system. Traditional economics has tried to confuse self-interest from greed, by portraying it as profit increase. However it goes without saying that this profit maximization has to be within the norms of acceptable behavior and the law. Just to quote some acts of outrageous greed from recent past of just one country USA, The Financial Times (2002) reported that as the 25 largest bankruptcies between 1999 and 2001 wiped out $210 billion in shareholder value and almost 100,000 jobs. Top management walked away with a combined $3.3 billion in compensation. In the same year, Fortune reported that executives and directors of 1,035 corporations pocketed $66 billion even as their company stock prices fell more than 75%. Paul Volcker, the former chairman of the Federal Reserve Board, commented that corporate greed exploded beyond anything that could have been imagined in 1990, an infectious greed seems to have gripped much of our business community, because —the avenues to express greed have grown so enormously. More recently, President Obama (2009) reflected on the attitude that's prevailed from Washington to Wall Street to Detroit for long; an attitude that valued wealth over work, selfishness over sacrifice, and greed over responsibility. Behavior on Wall Street may represent the most obvious, modern embodiment of this phenomenon.

Looking back into ancient human history, according to Sumerian and Greek mythology Atlantis was destroyed by the gods when greed and sin increased tremendously. The message of the story is applicable even today.

Although our planet is beautiful, some of the cities on our planet, especially in the developing world are incredibly messy and dirty. My spiritual interpretation of this phenomenon is that we are all children of the universe and mother earth – kind parents who allow their children to play and mess about in the play yard. Just as the play room of a naughty child can become very messy, we too as children of mother earth have messed up some of the spaces we have to play about in. Charged by greed, lust and pride, we have trampled on flowers and gardens of Nature. We suffer as a consequence of it. Father Universe permits that so that we may learn from suffering. It is time we grew up and co-operated with Nature in creating the same sort of beauty in our living areas as Nature does in parts of the planet where we have not yet had a chance to play and destroy. The developed parts of the world are facing a serious economic challenge. In order to overcome the crisis, causes of this recession have to be properly understood. Some of these are:

1. The resources of the earth have been exploited and this has resulted in an increase in the prices of commodities such as petroleum products. This directly impacts growth.

2. Governments have developed the habit of running deficit budgets and incurring debt in the hope that future growth would make debt repayment easy. If growth does not take place as is happening now this very debt becomes a burden impeding growth.

3. Essential institutions such as banks have been allowed a free hand to run on pure greed as against rational thinking and governments are now finding themselves at a loss as to how to deal with this. Perhaps humans can not be trusted enough to run banks privately and these need to be nationalized.

The US government has been talking of restoring the middle class through job creation. The proposed plans are not likely to work. Some of the reasons for this are:

A Brief Introduction

1. The new situation with high commodity costs (which will become even higher with time) is a new one. The old era of low resource costs has gone.

2. The new World trade arrangements are different.

3. Large stimulus and infrastructure spending as is being proposed by President Obama and economists of a bygone era will once again increase deficits and debt and thus prove to be counter productive.

One may wonder as to what the possible solutions to the economic crisis should be in the changing world. To this author's mind some of these are:

1. It has been said the protectionism is harmful. It is so, if it is done in a non-intelligent manner. There is a need for selective protectionism to increase jobs in developed countries. One tentative proposal is that when a trade deficit for goods and services, with any single country of the world is more than five percent (or some such figure) of the total trade volume (with all countries) during a year, a prohibitory duty on products from that country should be imposed for the following three years. The effect of this scheme would be that trade will continue freely with countries that do not cripple the economy and would get restricted with others that do. Things like garments would be made once again in the US and more jobs will be created. It will feel good where it matters if one knows that nimble fingers nearby have woven the underwear rather than in far way lands.

2. The future of mankind lies with diminishing size of cities and a partial return back to the land. The days of ever larger and larger cities is numbered. It was an unnatural phenomenon fuelled by low energy costs and a low earth population that will die its natural death in coming centuries. Governments can facilitate this process by creating small farm holding of about ten-acre size with a small two-room cottage (that may be expanded by the owner) on the dwelling and with roads, electricity and irrigation leading to these farms. A loan and knowledge may be provided to begin intensive farming operations with the farmland as collateral (that can always be allotted to a new farmer if need be).

3. Constitutional amendments need to be made to permit future deficit financing and debt only after a referendum and not as a routine. National budgets must be adjusted so that governments live within their means. The easiest way to do this is to divide the budget cut across all heads by the desired percentage.

4. There is an urgent need for government to control corporate barons and chief bankers to run away with the profits that belong to shareholders and the public. Top executive numerations must be capped as suggested in an earlier chapter and things like severance pay scrapped.

In the meantime the good news is that national debts have not compromised the future of our grandchildren. That future is already here in many countries and may not be far away in others. Learning from this experience, countries and individuals would have developed wiser debt free practices by the time the grandchildren grow up.

An Ominous Sign for Wasteful Economies

Although a scientist and engineer by profession, I have had deep interests in spiritualism and spiritual practices albeit tempered by scientific wisdom and logic. One of the side effects of this indulgence is that one develops certain symptoms and side effects that are similar to spiritualists of a more rigorous kind. I too have not been able to escape such symptoms and one of these is the reading of signs and occasional prophecy.

Thus, years ago when I served for a few years as a Professor of Mechanical Engineering in Saddam's Iraq, I noticed that the population throws away bagfuls of bread on a regular basis. This was before the gulf wars. One of the things that Saddam Hussein used to do to keep his subjects happy, besides the supply of fine European booze at subsidized rates, was the supply of near free bread through kiosks that were littered throughout Iraqi cities. The idea was that no citizen, howsoever poor, should go to bed on a hungry stomach. Booze was never thrown away. It improves on keeping and was consumed to the last drop even on the streets since Iraq was perhaps the only country in the world where public drinking was not illegal. On the other hand, citizens were quick to collect their bags of near free bread even when they did not need it. Soon enough unused bread goes dry and it was quickly discarded to the garbage bin. Noting this, I had a premonition that this was an evil sign and that it would soon be followed by a period of hunger and poverty in Iraq. It is nature's way of restoring balance through mechanisms that cannot be scientifically delineated or explained. Any resource that is misused and disrespected is eventually taken away through mysterious mechanisms of our wonderful universe albeit there may be a delay in this enforcing mechanism. It could be that the delay is mercy on the part of nature giving humans ample opportunity to mend their ways.

I returned to Canada then India well before the gulf war but followed the news on Iraq closely because I had so many dear friends in that country from the years I spent there. I noted with sadness that due to the war, sanctions and the disappearance of Saddam the population was facing hardships and hunger. Even bread had become scarce.

The papers had a report from the United Nations Environment Program that mentioned consumers throw away about 222 million tones of food in edible condition every year in the currently rich countries of North America and Europe. Approximately one third of the world's food goes waste and most of this wastage takes place in the presently rich countries. It is an ominous sign for the future. Is this wastage a sign of the impending shortages to occur in future? It is true that wastage in Europe began as far back as the ancient Greek civilization that introduced prosperity in Europe for the first time. The wastage was followed by the feasting binges of Rome. In recent years it seems that hunger has entered Athens and has begun to knock on the doors of Rome. Would this spread from here to shores far away or would others heed the warning signs in time.

Another ominous sign that is not difficult to understand scientifically is the adverse future impact of debt on personal as well as national economies. Presently the fixes that Europe is exploring involves taking more debt from elsewhere, China or perhaps by a Euro bond that would initially cost less than a Spanish or Italian bond. The developed economies need to learn from Estonia as to how to run a country without debt and grow. The fix that America is exploring is increasing more unsustainable consumption and perhaps more wastage. Traditional economists, locked into the existing unsustainable model of growth would love to see the wastage and retail sales go up.

State of Humans

We could divide all humans that live on our planet in three broad categories. Humans are not frozen into these categories but may move from one to another during a single life time. First are the rich and powerful. They are small in numbers but control and influence our world in major ways. Second are a group of humans who are neither exceptionally rich nor exceptionally powerful but they have enough financial means to acquire nutritious food for themselves and their family most times, comfortable dwellings to live in open surroundings filled with sunshine, fresh air and soothing greenery. Perhaps they may not have enough money to get a new Benz or a Ferrari but enough to get most things humans need to live and get along with. Then there is a third group of humans that is struggling to meet their daily needs, who have to frequently compromise on nutrition in food, The worst of this third category may even have to go hungry from time to time. There number on earth is not just in millions but billions at the present time. The combined wealth of three and a half billion of them are less than the wealth of just a hundred of the wealth of the humans described in the introductory chapter.

It is from amongst the second and middle category that the happiest and gentlest of humans are perhaps most likely to be found. The rich and powerful have too much to worry about and may create too much bad karma in order to acquire their wealth and power first and later to preserve and maintain it (leaving aside some saintly persons who rose from humble beginnings and retained their saintliness and some other rare cases that inherit that wealth or win a lottery yet retain their humility and simplicity as for example Queen Elizabeth and some other much loved European Royalty).

When the rich and powerful take a holiday from their strenuous schedules, it is too structured to be fun. They are hardly in a position to say, "This spot is so peaceful, I just love the lake and the weeping willows by the edge, let us hang on here for another week." On the other hand those from the struggling category have to struggle too much to acquire their daily bread. Happiness as available for free on the planet to all life may therefore escape both kinds. The few blessed and rare souls as mentioned in the previous paragraph however do not take off for a holiday but may go regularly to the same holiday home for generations, as for example Queen Victoria and even her descendents to the Balmoral Castle.

One may then try to see how those in the middle are doing. Not all who are in the middle category attain happiness even though they may have enough money for food etc. Some of them have compromised their happiness out of various desires like greed, lust, ego, worthless ambition that they shall discard only when their souls are withdrawn from their bodies by the Lord one day sooner or later to free them from their misery. They do work that they hate and have to commute too much on stress highway on a daily basis just to get on with their lives. At the present time many millions of them are compelled to live as an insect – a bee - in a dwelling stacked one above the other and side by side like a beehive, that a seller or renter conned them into saying that it is luxury or secure apartments with a million dollar view, or in a group of homes pushing into each other so as to block the sun and a whiff of fresh air from front, behind, left and one more side, in a city with much concrete and little greenery, where the air is laced with smog, smoke and too many farts (if you pardon the language) rather than the gentle song of birds and the scent of trees of the forest and wild flowers. The reason for being blunt about the state of such humans, very many millions of them is so that they may work to change the state they have got into, the first chance they get. These last from amongst the middle category are the condemned ones who deserve full sympathy of other humans even the poor because the poor may not have enough bread but they often have more peace and joy when they find that bread and laugh heartily later.

It is only few from the middle category, the gentle ones who have the freedom of mind and occupation to enjoy the many wonders of the beautiful side of our lovely planet, who are too meek to have too much ambition or to struggle for what they think rightly or wrongly should belong to them but rather content themselves with whatever comes with ease and joyous effort even if it is just a little, just enough to get by and a gift for the little girl who lives down the lane. It is they who have inherited the earth along with a few others from the rich and powerful category as described in the exceptions of this category and a few others that are poor and might live in a mud hut yet do not have to struggle for their daily needs as described in the links of the previous paragraph.

In conclusion, it is neither the possession of wealth and status nor even a lack of it that wins happiness and evolution for a soul but simplicity and humility along with love and compassion for all life including the green side of it, the meekness to be contented with what life gives without a struggle and a fight, those whose hearts have not yet hardened from the many knocks none but they themselves gave to it perhaps because of their lusting, anger, stupid pride, constant quarrels, arguments etc. with those near enough to them to permit it, who have retained the love, compassion and wisdom to do their bit to improve their own lives and the world around them in whatever way the Lord made them capable for it, that helps a human to come out a winner and inherit the earth. Principles of economics have to be compatible with these basic principles of humanism to be sustainable over the long term.

The Future for all

Even in the best of democracies on our planet it seems that a select group of persons control wealth and power because it seems that 99 per cent of the wealth of a country is controlled by much less than one percent of the population. The wealthiest of persons are able to continue with relatively low rates of taxes and the wealthiest of bankers are able to get away with millions of dollars in compensation, even if they cause a national financial crisis whereas a struggling construction worker loses his home mortgage even after back breaking hours of labour. Politicians are able to successfully argue or enforce that the poorest of the population that may be struggling with food should not be given basic medical treatment by the state to avoid pain and suffering for themselves and their children if they cannot afford it. In countries such as India there is a system of party whip where a single party leader is able to issue a dictate to vote to all of the public representatives as he or she thinks right, and not as per their conscience or constituents, leading to a concentration of power in a few hands.

It may be argued that humans have evolved. A democratic government is obliged to introduce welfare measures in order to ensure votes. However even in monarchies welfare measures were common or monarchs ended up without their heads as Marie Antoinette of France. However, humans have evolved to the point that power has spread out from one to at least one percent. With further evolution it is hoped that it will spread from one percent to ten percent, twenty percent, and thirty percent and eventually to all.

While there is a good and bad side to just about everything in the universe with the exceptions of God and the Devil, there are things that add more evil than good and others that contribute more good than evil and ugliness to the world. Internet is one human invention that is already helping to eradicate evil from the world and would continue to do so over the next several decades and centuries.

Why is that? The simple answer to that is – evil prospers in the dark, when information is suppressed and lies and false argument such as those put out by private banks with profiteering managements can be maintained whereas truth is bright and prevails as information flows freely. The several million dollar salary of rich bankers is to prevent loss of talent and the politicians can do nothing about it except make polite noises about the stench which does not vanish even with a forty thousand dollar commode on Wall Street. The bankers on the other hand say it is just to prevent the flight of talent. However, one must accept one's own responsibility for the state of affairs. We elected them after all.

Since when did a greedy pig like being with the head and bottom of a human become talented, and if a political ruler is unable or unwilling to limit the size of a bank that is too big to fail or to limit the salary of an executive that is too big to swallow, would the people have to elect the fairy godmother to rule over them instead?

And,

Just as a hungry man saying some food is bad makes more sense than a man stuffed with food saying so; it makes more sense if a poor person says taxing the rich is bad than a man stuffed with wealth. The tragedy with persons who lie or argue with a vested interest is that they do it so often that they start believing in the lie for as long as the Lord keeps them in the long waiting line to the bottomless pit.

There has been no greater tool than the Internet in helping to make information available freely to just about anyone. It is true that humans enjoying privileges do not easily give those up and when they also have power at their command they will naturally fight the loss of privilege, even if it is an evil and unjust one. Thus it is not surprising if some countries attempt to ban parts of the internet or even in the most extreme case the entire internet access from the public, something that can happen only in the most extreme form of dictatorship in the world. In fact the extent to which internet access is curbed in different countries of the world or the truth-seers hounded is an extent of the measure of its lack of democracy despite what it might portray or claim in public and conversely also the extent of the poverty and/or distress of its masses even though the wealth of rich exploiters and dictators may be immense in such countries with widespread poverty.

Thus whereas religion has not succeeded in freeing the world of evil because religious leaders themselves became corrupt and whereas neither communism nor capitalism has been able to free the world from the yoke of the exploiting one percent (which in reality is one percent of one percent of one percent) a change may come about merely through the medium of the internet. A change that will not come in a day or a year or even decades but bit by evil shall be exposed and then banished making the planet more just and beautiful.

www.ingramcontent.com/pod-product-compliance
Lightning Source LLC
Chambersburg PA
CBHW071755170526
45167CB00003B/1035